Songs of a Word Weaver

Words woven from
half a century's songs
of wonder, love,
heartache, heartbreak,
change, ageing, illness,
and the endless quest
for this journey's purpose.
Heart worn on a sleeve,
spun from intertwining reels
of vibrant, silken thread,
unfettered, but vulnerable.
Mind wired with taut,
unforgiving strands,
cutting deep with
undeniable reason.
Turn the pages, if you will,
and travel with me across
a story-telling tapestry,
draping once naïve walls
with a life's rich experience.

Songs of a Word Weaver

By

Keith M. Kendrick

ISBN: 978-1-7395230-1-5

Photo credit: NightCafe (https://creator.nightcafe.studio/)

DEDICATION

I thank my families in both in the UK and China for their continuous support in my life both as a scientist and as a poet and the many people across the world whose lives have touched mine and inspired my thoughts and words.

CONTENTS

PREFACE

I am a scientist, although I never set out to be. I never even dreamed of being one when I was young and didn't take science options at school. I am a creator, dreamer, and explorer who almost imperceptibly drifted away from the emotional uncertainty of art towards the more tangible excitement of discovery in the realm of hard science. There was also, of course, the small but highly influential and deciding matter of career, money, and even emotional stability. Just how many poets have ever been successful in obtaining some, or indeed any, of these?

But the world keeps turning, careers are made, falter, and are revived; reputations are slowly won and quickly lost; discoveries are written into the record for human posterity. However, all the time our essential nature remains waiting to be rediscovered when an unexpected revolution finds the face it thought was hidden is visible again. So it has been with me and poetry.

The poems in this collection were, therefore, written in distinct and very different phases of my life: between thirteen and twenty-six and then in the years after I turned fifty, arguably at the peak of my scientific career as a professor but with a broken marriage and a new and uncertain emotional life again. These two things enriched my life, tore me apart, and finished with me leaving Cambridge in the UK and starting a new life in Chengdu, China. Arguably it is through my time in China that I have managed to discover my chi in time to both embrace the challenges of old age and pursue my true scientific ambition of trying to develop new therapies for mental illness well beyond my expected age of retirement. Chengdu describes itself as the city where dreams come true and where people never want to leave after they have experienced its lifestyle. I resonate with both of these sentiments. The poems in the collection are all undoubtedly in the romantic tradition and reflect a distillation of the influence that nature, love, rejection, dreams, experience, religion, aging, and death can have on both emotion and intelligence. Through them, the poems derive a sense of identity, purpose, and meaning. In short, they are a collection of thoughts and emotions woven into verse, stretching from where I am now and where I have been in the past to where a future might or might not lead. More than anything else, they are a celebration of emotion, both good and bad, and of language expressed and spun in both the constraints and the freedoms that are intrinsic to the brevity and power of poetry.

The poems are organised thematically rather than historically, although the reader will probably surmise when they were written from the different styles and sentiments expressed. The illustrations are generated by AI (NightCafé) using words from some of the poems.

NATURE, ART, AND REMEMBRANCE

A WALK IN THE PARK

The air is heavy, odour-torn
with blossom-sprinkled, sweat-soaked grass,
and petalled trees dipped in the spawn
that bathes new life with droplet glass,
full brimmed in morning's scent-brushed swathes
of warmth and honeyed, rose-lipped haze.

Colours spread in saffron light
of rising sun and flesh-tinged sky,
infuse each scene with gifted sight,
flooding all other worlds run dry
with sucking thoughts and blotted past,
each vision drunk as though my last.

No human tongue to break this round
of nature's calls, whose chattered song
plays urgent music's fluted sound,
reverberates all morning long,
clamouring food for throated nests,
bursting with life that never rests.

Fine-dusted breeze thrills every pore
of down-blown skin and brimming eye,
floating my senses through their door
to leave each care a passerby,
who walks into this spring-flushed dawn
where night's undone and hope's reborn.

THE COLOURS OF EVENING

Damasked evening
spreads in liquid furls
of rich, burnt ochre.
Breeze-billowed shadows
brush olive wheat
and saffron rape,
birch trees caught
in silvered rush
of leaf-whispered sound
and played by dancing,
outstretched fingers
of a zephyr wind.

No other body
shares this view
of darkening sunset,
mixed with cloud-flecked
pastel blue of whited day.
The daylight colours
in each painted scene,
which basked in floods
of bright, translucent light
bathed now by grown eclipse,
in dusky setting pink,
slow-painted by a bolder,
more-impressioned brush,

with pallet fired
by the tinctures
of a sinking orb
falling, russet-deep,
into the emptiness
of this nightfall's
western sky.

ROBINS

A slow, relentless tidal surge
that splashes winter's coat of white
with flecks of multicoloured spume,
caught dancing in the growing light.
The swirling, iridescent flume
of breathless hope and restless urge
releasing thoughts our lives submerge.

All this has placed you in my tree,
a small, unlikely flashing thrust
of red, plucked from a grey-blue sky,
whose clouds obscure the jealous lust
that keeps your partner's roving eye—
Watching your strutting, preening spree,
encircling you, ignoring me.

Her shadow catches your display,
disturbs your momentary pride
with nervous wings and shifting feet
that call her swiftly to your side,
so you can touch her neck and greet
those willing eyes that light your day,
hinting mischievousness and play.

I wonder where you'll be tonight,
whose tree will feel your nervous tread,
whose eye will glimpse you by the moon
and see your feathers bathed in red?
Morning will reunite us soon
to contemplate this winter's flight,
in shards of effervescent light.

FIRST DAY OF AUTUMN

Cold, damp, attention-seeking air
surrounds the vitals of my calm,
with threatened chill of season's care.
No breezy softness of summer balm
or aroma of perfumed heat,
this morning's taste is bittersweet.

Trees shed their first dead messengers,
slow spun in free spiralling fall.
Ground beckons the floating dancers
with wetness of a dew-dropped squall,
grasps in clammy outstretched fingers,
one last breath—life's beauty lingers.

LEAF GAZING

My care succumbs
to forest sound,
rustling whispers
swirling round.

Thick canopies
of writhing leaves,
spun in the breeze—
tangled wreaths.

Pressed round my head,
their dancing, blind,
crowds this mossy bed,
spins my mind.

Green-swathed caress
softer than a breast,
whose gossamer dress
floats, skin-caressed.

Their bright life giver
drifting into view,
formed in a blur
of morning dew.

Tears brim my eye,
too dry from staring
at a leaf-tossed sky,
lost with seeing.

INSIDE A PAINTING

His flanks are tense,
his head is proud,
his destination vain.
None question will he jump the fence
or if he fears the leaden cloud
which threatens pounding sheets of rain.

The rider's thighs
can sense his steel,
taut muscles driving bone.
He only hears her piercing cries,
the tearing pain that spurs his heel,
all other feeling turned to stone.

The cloudburst falls,
and droplets spill
to swell a torrid stream.
But nothing drowns her dying calls,
not surging tide, nor sudden thrill
of pounding hoof and anxious scream.

Joint echoes stun
the bridge below,
which groans from sudden weight
as man and beast strain to outrun
life's quick-spent forces they must know
will make their journey's end too late.

This hanging noise
of artist's toil
that shocks or even shames,
quiet brought through canvas-painted poise
with colour, brush, and scented oil
in rooms of varnish-tinted frames.

MIDNIGHT SEA

Midnight sea lapping at my feet,
ink caressed by pallid moon streams,
the night-scape rousing bittersweet
remembrance of youthful star beams,
when I had shared their thousand eyes
in times of carefree, cloudless skies.

Wind enticing with rippled calm,
dares each traveller venture deep
beyond life's soft-shelled, sandy balm,
keeping doubts safe in gritted sleep.
What hope will our tomorrow turn
the tides of yesterday's concern?

They say moon gazing drives men mad,
but I have seen too many sane
whose light was snuffed before they had
the chance to twist their hopes in pain
and lose their grip in clinging sand
that moulds each step upon life's strand.

A JAPANESE SHRINE

I feel an ancient quiet
descending on the remnants
of my punch-blown mind,
caught in its millstone
where petty circumstance
grinds out the consequence
of caring too much.

The cultural peace of
long-dead civilization,
denizens of followers
who lived another code
and spoke another tongue,
filling the air with
remembrance of time.

Locked in every screen
and crafted pagoda,
with dark satin wood
and gilded tile.
Immortality
set in a tableau
of ornamental greenery,
water, and sculpted sand.

The temple bell
sounds its solemn call,
echoing through ordered
paddy fields and
peaceful ornament
of tended gardens.

Here human hand
is like the breeze
that busies life
upon each sod
of hallowed ground
but leaves no mark
to break the calm
and willing sleep
of ancestors.

WAR MEMORIAL

Erect on a squall-struck, moss-torn hill
it stands—death's memory in shade.
A solitary bedraggled wreath
lies at its centre, a yellow splash
in a green-slate world of plant and stone.

Why is it here on this barren crest?
Looking out on swathes of tangled bracken,
driving down on scattered firs and rocks,
breaking with the morning's unveiling
on a vast but empty, eddied lake.

Is it for us to remember them
or a focal point to congregate?
Not in some famous, foot-trodden street
or town square bustling with noisy throats
but in still, natural emptiness.

Nothing living settles here for long.
Both forgiving and unforgiving,
it well reflects the sacrificial
elements consumed in water, land,
and sky that once held their souls in warmth.

Small groups worn by the climb huddle round,
sharing small, lesser thoughts of conquests
where nothing of consequence was risked.
The rising wind tosses shallow words
away from your silent edifice.

A thin sun breaking thickening clouds
spreads, flowing light across the hills,
revealing threaded streams and copses.
Reaching your weathered pinnacle,
casting time's far-travelled shadow.

Time has little meaning in this place,
just past reflection of what was once
life ignorant of eternity.
Now death, as each year's wind-tossed flowers
wilt before this war's unflinching face.

FIRST AND
UNREQUITED LOVE

FIRST LOVE

Such passion in a timid kiss
might well have locked
that long and weary grasp
which time keeps on her children.
But love was just a game of pride
that ended once between the sheets
and left us there for ever;
faint hearts grow sadly old,
so aged by that first sorrow.
Now walking by a lake at night,
I see your face within the face
that now I love, and crying softly
in my heart, remember then
those tears shed feebly on the ground
when once we knew young love could lie—
not me and you, but I…and I.

ONE-NIGHT STANDS

There will not be a warmer clime
to catch spring beauty in their eyes,
for all is timeless, frozen soil,
lust a relentless pendulum
to furrow-curve the frosted ground.

Draped virginal in social white,
this cold defiance of the heat
lies resolute in natural scorn of life
and slowly numbs the skin
with pallid afterthoughts
of sheeted forms of closet love,
confined to other worlds than this
in vacant boarding houses
huddled by a writhing sea.

Exposed above the wave-beat lie
tomorrow's lovers whispering...
"Today a scented rose escaped
the bitter salt-spray of our lives."
And though an attic darkness
obscures the knowledge of their hours,
each morning still betrays the sense
in pressing faded flowers.

In memory of one-night stands,
the lighthouse rises through the seas,
in church the vicar reads the banns,
while curtains flutter in the breeze.

UNREQUITED LOVE

Across the room a candle burns,
cold spirit of a dying flame—
alone upon a wasteland.

Slumped among distorted shadows
with eyes half-closed by drink,
my dreams have twisted in the light
that threads her picture on the wall,
and I have listened,
listened for her footstep in the hall.

Or walking on a street at night,
I recognise a figure lit
in the deep and empty pool
of amber thrown around a face
and then looked again
to see a stranger take her place.

Or lying sprawled across a bar,
I hear her voice call softly,
call out above the raucous crowd.
But as my stupor quickly clears,
I stare about my ears deceived,
my smoke-filled eyes half blind with tears.

Or drunk, returning to my room,
I contemplate a hopeless love
and watch her silent face appear
within the sharp blue-fingered flame,
and wonder,
wonder if she knows my name.

Or when she beckons me to wake
and move her with a laughing kiss,
I stretch and blow her face away;
for in the flame a dreamer's mind
can see her still,
but know what it can never find.

Across the room a candle dies,
cold remnant of a lifeless flame—
alone upon a wasteland.

FOR A FRIEND

No, the mirror does not lie
in what it shows of you.
Your face today will fill
the eyes that look upon
your eyes and ask for nothing.

Nor nothing in return,
but one faint smile
that enters once in every heart
where it remains forever...

Yes, even mine.

But soon the dance must end,
and you must be as one of us,
unnoticed by the passing eyes.
Then hold the mirror up again
and try the steps
that once could tease us all...
Again the mirror will not lie;
and when its truth torments
your footsteps on the darkened stage,
draws out the dying moments
in a breathless and impassioned dance,

pray that your dreams live out
vague memory of hurtful words
which dared speak out of things
half buried by hypnotic trance.

Then, wait the timid hush that falls
upon the echoes of applause,
and remember it was only I,
not time, saw fit to strip away
the beauty from your flashing eyes,
beyond false subtlety and grace,
behind the curtain of your face.

DOG DAY'S PASSION

If only they had seen
sunset drool on a counterpane
or felt the salivating nerve
draw taut a twisted smile,
they might, at an untidy pause,
have snared the taunted beast
with scorn or sympathetic barb.
But nothing spoke; nothing moved,
or saw those ugly tears, brim, swell,
slip, slide, fall on faded patches
smothered in the half-light.

Stung by imaginings,
lust in crimson eddies quivers,
hovering on spit-moistened jowls,
swimming with deceptive creases,
passion heaves its final prelude.
Tearing claws discretely ribbon
letters cursed and not forgiven.

The face alone remains,
posing a taut frivolity
with studied, predatory guile,
betraying false perfection's curve
and broken promise in a look.
Eyes show hints of female nightmare,

a modest unobtrusive nose,
shocked hair startled by a sunburst,
but knowing not to hide her face.
Abandon gleams through parted lips
and would have spoken of a smile
if the shutter hadn't fallen,
thin bright, angled fragments
latticing her startled face,
lengthening the jagged shadows,
closing in on the sagging head,
growling this one last memory.

THE HEALER

He is the Healer,
bringer of lotus balm
and silken sleep.
The steady voice
plunging steel
into scaly throated
Demons,
muting their scream.
The boundless soul
to whom
can pass all pain
and trauma
by taking
as his own.
The spirit whose
silent love
need never
be spoken
beyond cure.

A Love that binds
each reaching hand
to heal the souls
of damaged Angels,
drawn to the light
of his embrace.

A Love that is
pure energy
of purpose,
until healing
seals the portal
of its care.

A Love that flows
to all who
open their heart,
consume his words,
and feel the zephyr's
soothing whisper
breathing calm across
distance and time.

He is the bringer
of others' dreams,
dreams that never
can be his.

For he is nothing
but the wind
blowing in the
lonely vastness
of a mystic ocean,

filling torn sails
of passing ships
until they're gone
where they are bound,
and he is become
the memory
of salty tears
grown sweet upon
each Angel's face.

He is the Healer,
condemned to wander
this storm-broken,
hungry sea
of shipwrecked souls
who seek direction
in his journey's light,
and, by their
safe passing,
fill his beacon's
raging emptiness.

TO A MERMAID

My heart told me she loved me—
but loved another more,
not as we loved, but different,
a love from another shore.
A shore that gave her comfort,
a shore that filled her dreams,
not storm-tossed in her little boat
but warm, calm, and serene.

I wondered she still loved me,
there seemed no reason why.
Though she could only answer:
He was her choice, not *I*.

Now with every sunset
she gazes out to sea,
and dreams the storm
that found her heart,
calling once more to me.
But she was too long coming,
her boat too often beached,
my love lost to an ocean floor
no mermaid ever reached.

IN MEMORIAM

When romance holds an empty stair
that stretches upwards to my room,
and pictures shape quiescent hours
with softer hopes of sculpted clay,
then tender hands may mould a face
forgotten through ambitious years
of books and dismal passion.

Some young admirer may then praise
this final vision of my life,
and all will love the perfect dream
that broke my harsher effigies
on pedestals of famous hate.

Should students threaten to reveal
your name and flaunt it in the street,
then I may force a lonely smile
and press my finger to your lips
to keep the silence of a heart
that whispers all that it might do
in memory of loving you.

SUPERMARKET LOVE

I'm smitten with a churlish maid
thinks Waitrose better than getting laid,
who spurns an orgasm's shuddered thrill
for queueing at the checkout till,
encounters with the fruit and veg
preferred to reaching passion's edge.
How can I know if meat's her dish?
I could be beef, and she'd want fish!
Or if I turned to shrimp terrine,
her eyes might yearn for langoustine.
Do steamed concoctions make her boil,
or is she stirred by olive oil?
I'd lure her to the dairy aisle
if whipping cream would her beguile.
How can I beat her trolley dash?
No discount here for paying cash!
I'll have to join the retail trade
if all my hope's not doomed to fade.
Then using my best bargain voice…
tempt her with the manager's choice!

IN LOVE

WHY DO WE LOVE?

Why do we love...you've always asked?
Because we simply have no choice,
our seed must propagate its seed.
So love is grown from primal need;
attraction spawns its fatal brood
and brings a wild, impulsive mood.

But have you ever wondered why
you feel empty when love is done,
its madness past, its fever run?
You know without it you can't find
a better cause to fill your mind.

And the irony then, of course,
is ending back where you began,
remaking chains to fetter love,
watching others wearing its glove,
catching their voices, breathing sighs
lost from lips that can only mouth
sounds you dare not make or hear,
or mist your eye with lover's tear.

But left alone its song will hue
a growing cleft inside of you,
aching with each remembered sound
and voice you've smothered underground.
A Siren's call you least expect,
that drives all mad who love neglect.

IN AND OUT OF LOVE

My love lay with me on a bed,
her kisses warm remembered lips
touched by delicate fingertips
transforming every word unsaid.

She spoke of love that came with ease,
its passion obviating choice,
but words soon found a pleading voice,
"Why don't, why can't you, sorry, please!"

Words force-intended to join her
in a place our hearts couldn't be;
our love would turn soundless and bitter,
so though guilt remains, we are free.

LOVE SLEEPING

Night closes in once more
on four grim walls
that bear their epitaph,
where shadows creep
like ivy over brick
which, left untended,
obscures the eyes
of this historic room,
as now mine are tired
with being open.

Now only reverie
awakens love,
and dreams delight
my fitful sleep
with fantasies of worlds
where we are not confined
by time, or place,
or even memories
that crowd this room,
and resurrect the pulse
where feelings shocked
dead brick with life.

So solid fabric
can sense once more
the deeper presence
of a love that thrilled
this winter's passion,
dancing in its shadow,
even as the one
that lengthens
on the walls
of this, my prison,
as I prepare to sleep
and dream the life
where time and
ghosts depart
and we awake,
together.

Night closes in once more
on four grim walls
that bear their epitaph
where shadows creep,
like ivy over brick
which, still untended,
closes the eyes
of this historic room

where love once slept
and dared each passerby
to look within
and leave without
a moment's envy.

ECHO

There are no words that can express
your love's exquisite tenderness,
that feeling when your looks beguile
and steal my senses with their smile.
Each moment looking through your eyes
reveals a hidden truth's disguise,
your mouth as honest as its lips
that kiss my outstretched fingertips.
This leaving brings such emptiness,
each heartbeat's brooding loneliness.
The world's a cold and dreary place
without your kindred soul's embrace.
Two lives whose distant echoes found
two voices with a single sound.

A FIRST GOODBYE

Now is the moment when its face
becomes visible to my mind,
a rush of sudden vacant space
fast-filled by tears, my eyes half blind
with stinging oceans of despair,
caught in their sweeping waves where loss
seems all, though joyous white caps toss
their hope this tide won't drag us there.

We walk, heavy with care of time,
streets emptied by our soon goodbye,
but noisy with the cheerless crime
of talking, though it's lifeless tone
tells more than words could ever hide.
Our hands guide softly in their thread
towards the nearer end we dread,
tensed bodies losing warmth inside.

And then we stop where feet arrived,
their final journey corners thought
that might have led us back inside.
But now turned outward, movement caught
with its certainty of an end
brought closer by time's urgent cause
to break this passage through its pause.
Our eyes close messages they send.

Now blindness gently opens lips,
their skin inflames elation lost
and pulls us tight, as touching slips
to breathless parting's final cost
of stifling air that let us be
a presence framed by shadow-play,
brushed through with colours of a day
that lit one brief eternity.

ABSOLUTE LOVE

I feel the taste of your lips,
the smell of your hair,
your eyes locked deep
within my every waking dream,
your fingers touching everywhere,
playing on my skin,
pulling at my heart.
Your face is the only face I see,
your voice in every voice I hear
until there is nothing else,
nothing else worth sensing.
You are the only air I can breathe.
There are no thoughts
that do not become you.

A LOVER'S BREEZE

My thought rides eddied by the breeze
to gently agitate and tease
your sultry calm of afternoon.
Its evening wings then speck the moon
with darting shadows chasing light,
their forms picked out in soundless flight,
displacing air, which swirling free,
swells waves of shivered ecstasy.
Reverberates your waking skin
with rhythms touching deep within,
their pleasure held by faint caress
of soft, exquisite tenderness
that flutters with your heart's unrest,
its feathers brush each rising breast.
Returns each morning, flushed with care,
my presence felt—though never there.

HANDS ACROSS THE PARK

The New York winter sun
has risen in your east
and will set in my west
for this one longest day.
A world shrunk to a patch
of wooded arbours
where souls can meet
and find their willing flesh.

This snow-cloaked park
is all that lies between,
its crooked, spinstered trees,
naked from abandoned leaves,
are veiled and downed with
the frost-caked confetti
of fleeting bridal relief.

Your seventieth to
my eighty-first,
with many roads and
twisted paths between.
Though none where line of sight
is lost to break our gaze.

Your brown, my blue,
their two philosophies
deep liquid pools
of trust that beggar words,
though we will speak them
because we must
to be ourselves.

Words that will bind us
where we linger hand in hand,
conjoined by thoughts
and then full lips,
warmed by this local sun
which will change the paths
that drove us north from south,
and bring our distant souls,
lost in their wandering,
together at their zenith.

A LOVER'S PROMISE

I'll be your only fantasy,
the centre point that is your soul.
Each thought, each idle fancy,
each dream you dream to make you whole.

Be everywhere your mind can look,
your spirit in my heart's embrace.
Your joy will be my only book,
each word the smile upon your face.

You are the star that is my truth,
which never leaves the morning sky.
The fountain that is all my youth,
where I must drink or surely die.

LOVE'S ELEMENTAL FLAME

There was a time
I knew only thrill
of body aching
from its heart's desire,
but now the glass
of passing years
reflects the image
of another fire—
more powerful yet
than any heat
could burn before.
An elemental flame
to light recesses
of studied minds
and teases all outward
passion with its game,
played out in thought,
in act, in touch,
flash-joined as one
all future long,
married with a glance
of knowing eyes,
that sees our hope
eternal in its song.

WORDS THAT MAKE MEN DREAM

Speak conjured words to weave this dream
that spins your hope around my heart.
Though silence rushes us apart,
its sinews merely thread their stream,
blood pounding with each eddied sound,
life pulsed by thoughts your love has found.

Speak words whose waking drowns my sleep
with sudden promises you'll keep.
Words cast beyond slow reason's guile
and words to make me dream your smile.

AN UNINVITED GUEST

It's early, far too soon
to make an entrance.
An empty-handed,
uninvited guest
brushing off
uncertainty and cold.
The New York wind
has emptied your street
of all but a doorman
and a lone, shuffling hobo.
Other humanity
locked deep inside,
their shutters closed
and curtains drawn.

I've passed your door
four times at least,
wondering what thoughts
of this forced encounter
you might have?
…Or perhaps none at all?
A favour to repay,
a substituted evening
to sound a hollow time
your better, knowing friend
should have filled

with their music and love,
instead of sending me...
a promissory note.

I am nothing to you
but, being nothing,
there can be discovery
through equal, open minds
whose lives can share
the cumulative honesty
of their experience.

And even bodies too...
there is that chance.
I know I am rejected
by a more familiar mouth
whose lips betrayed me
with their ambivalence
only yesterday,
wounds too fresh perhaps
to let feelings in again.

It's the appointed time,
the front lock buzzing
with impatient release
as my voice finds reply.

I wait at your door,
which opens onto
upturned, curious eyes.
I step inside your space,
watching you move
to where we must begin,
knowing from that brief
first-entered moment
some part of me
will not be leaving.

DON'T DENY OUR LOVE

My darling,
don't deny our love;
it came from nowhere
but our hearts.
Now it's settled
in our touch
and every thinking
moment's breath;
there is no ending
but together,
our bodies joined
through loving will,
caught in each touch
and shuddered thrill.

We will not find
another sea
whose storms can set
our passions free.
So now we've found
each other's heart,
there simply is
no life apart.

ABSENT LOVE

In the absence of your words,
my thoughts fly aimlessly
and cannot find their rest.
Afraid to touch your earth,
they circle in your sky,
air breathed through memory,
time slowly rushing by.

IF ONLY YOU WOULD

If only you would,
no moment's regret,
no looking back,
no duty or distance
could prevent us.

If only you would
run naked into the rain,
just to feel yourself wet;
thaw off the snow
in my firelight's
warm embrace;
feel your skin tingle
as I kiss your face.

Life is where *we* are,
not hanging on hooks
or waiting in the wings.
Here as we prepare for
each new entrance's hope,
spoken loud in between
each carefully chosen word.

Here in each skilful pirouette
danced with wistful promises.
Danced until our steps run wild
on wanting's canted stage.
Lost in the tottering,
helpless tangle
of one unguarded look,
all acting dissembled,
falling off reason's edge onto
uncertainty's precipice.

A FIRST KISS

We sit closer, with thoughts touching,
willing some accidental gesture
brings brief contact that can linger
into promised intimacy.

Eyes locked, then quickly averted
when longing is too obvious.
Fingers turned to twist
a nervous stem whose
brimming glass is filled with
deep intention seeking,
sipped with fretful, lip-wet kisses
that crave another mouth was pressed
with taste more delicate than grapes...
but far more intoxicating.

Then sudden movement steals the gap
it seemed only chance could close
and lays my hand on parted legs,
joined by a hand that grips my own.
So we begin...unsure at first
if meaning lay in what happened.
Fingers released in emphasis
but soon creeping back together,

comfortable in the growing warmth
of desire beneath their touch...
our conversation still banal.

Then this polite absurdity
shattered with the shocking demand
for a kiss!
Given!
No question asked...
or answered.
A darting peck,
over before its warmth had time
to register in my senses,
but pulled into repetition,
a longer press with open mouth,
lips swollen and flushed,
the taste of probing tongues,
a thrusting, swooping need
that shatters glass
and empties all resistance.

LOVER'S DAWN

You are gone,
walking on lines
enforcing return
to a life these many
years has made
so safe, so dull.
No breathless passion
as this evening,
bruising our lips
in the moonlight
of an empty street.

A quick glance back—
Have I gone inside?
Did I see your
uncertain movement,
where you would have
run back to me?
…No surely not.
You look downwards,
eyes afraid of what
was seen in mine.
Your hair dishevelled
by fingers and kisses,
lips puffed with their
frantic desire to please.

Your back still burning
with the crude impression
of my searching hands
that threatened lower,
beyond and beneath
the gartered, flimsy lace
of feminine pride.
Pride I had known
all along was hidden
below each flowing
sashay of hip and dress.

Faster now,
feet falling to the
rhythm of your street,
door beckoning safety.
Opens with a push
of trembling hands
still warm with mine.

You step inside,
surrounded by sounds
of familiar home,
their comfort drained
by growing thoughts
this night could

have led to those
long-worn secrets
finding discovery
and exquisite purpose,
breath choked with
craving touch
and arching need
that beggars sleep
with lovers' dawn.

NOW IS THE TIME

Now is the time
your heart must choose
what its beat can't lose,
what its hope can't climb.

Does its pulsing feel
the loss absence brings,
to empty those things
each want can reveal?

Does it swell your tears
from thoughts that I've born,
your face tense and drawn
with stopping its fears?

Does it ask each day
why has it returned
to comforts you've learned,
play rhythms that stay?

Or can it break loose,
its essence torn free,
to risk life with me
and slip comfort's noose?

Time threatens our fate,
tossed in its passing,
turning on the ring
whose promise came late.

SILENT DECEPTION

My words speak back the silent voice
that turns your face so you won't hear
the telling sigh and ready tear
that stains your face with safety's choice.
What you have felt still trapped inside
the love your body's cast aside.

How could you want a man so much
you've known less than a moment's space?
Scarce time to find his true embrace.
Yet you remember every touch
that played your heart and drove you wild
with wanting, pleading like a child.

You have a life worn with its song,
so every day is filled with noise
that satisfies the careful poise
you've sculpted over decades long.
But when you lie each night in bed,
it's thoughts of me that crowd your head.

My hands mould every part of you
from tender memory of hours
spent locked in hotel rooms and bars
and threaten all the things you do
to block my face, my words, my kiss,
my love, and yours—you can't dismiss.

Now even sounds your lips won't make
sing hope that you will light my day
with every glance and word you'd say.
Accept our love for loving's sake;
tell me the truth; you can't deceive,
and I will never, ever leave.

BEYOND DESIRE

We lie together exhausted,
flesh burning from our love making,
hearts pounding with coarse passions fed
by a hungry, fevered thrusting
that scores each loving, never done
with fusing two of us as one.

Pleasure screams through swollen lips
where I have torn inside your flesh.
Now slow, gyrating fingertips
caress flushed skin as bodies mesh
in tight embrace while breathing slows;
eyes meet where feeling overflows.

How many times our wanting spent
have taken us beyond desire?
Now this has made such need absent
and moved to sense another fire
that burns more slowly, deep into
each tiny move and spark of you.

I feel the pulse that makes your life,
each sigh, each gesture that you do.
I see the woman as a wife
and me forever part of you.
Your hair, your scent, your every touch,
my heart could never want so much.

FALLING IN LOVE

We stand quiet, touching only through
silky wetness of wine-sipped lips,
bodies held close with thrusting flow
of eager pressing fingertips,
resting on nape and arching greed,
forced by our passion's restless need.

Eyes probing deep in what they know
will be our last love-making's chance
to take us where we should not go,
beyond our simple lover's dance.
Take us so we are joined as one,
beyond where wanton pleasure's done.

Before has just been craving rush
of want and shuddered ecstasy,
broken by drink and smoke-filled hush,
where talking gives proximity
to minded hearts our sex out-ran
towards an end we didn't plan.

We move, silent, clasped hands dictate
the ground where we must lay our spore
on whitened sheets, whose crumpled fate
shows times where we have failed before

to grow us into love that stays,
beyond these games lust always plays.

This time a feel whose eager flame
licks through our being, claiming all,
caught up in throats loose with desire
but calmer with each rise and fall
of bodies swept by burning heat,
now lying still, crushed and replete.

No break this time for smoke or drink,
no time to dress, or call an end,
no need to talk, or even think;
time now has finished to pretend
that it is over—just begun
to bind two elements as one.

This moment when we fell in love
will never pass where we forget.
Our senses breathe damp flesh above
the perfumed scent of lover's sweat,
joining two hearts our bodies keep,
their beating slowing into sleep.

I watch you dream and stroke your hair
and whisper words not used before.
Sometimes you wake and burrow where
your head can find its cradled shore.
So much complete, so soft and slight,
the words "I love you" end our night.

EVERYTHING

Your voice is controlled,
relaxed but uncertain
of where my hands
will wander next.
Talking as a friend
and listening to my words
as if entranced
by their meaning.

But you don't resist,
almost ignoring
my touch on your thighs,
my burning look of love
directed at your eyes
that pulls you up
onto my lips
and caresses between
your guarded sex.

All sense of calm
and poise abandoned
in frantic desire,
buried into flesh
like rutting animals.

Knowing every moment
could be the last
to make a memory
that defines *us*.

Your mouth locks
into my skin,
tearing in its
desperation for release
from wanting
more than you can bear.
Towards a shattered,
shuddering climactic
essence of charge
shocking all
sense of humanity
with its surge.

Wild in its call
to senses other life
can never touch,
never dream,
except together
in this room
where all was lost
but briefly found.

The very meaning
of our existence,
a pleasure never
to be matched
unless we hear
another sound
whose song plays
rhapsodies
no instrument
can ever match
without our bodies.

Without our ecstasy,
without our love
that stretches every
sinew of our being,
leaves us complete,
together in the calm
that says nothing…
but means everything.

BECOMING US

I wake your every morning,
my touch fills every night.
You never leave my thinking;
you are my only light.

I find what you keep hidden,
a woman deep and wild.
You find my darkest prison
and free this man's lost child.

I am your every sunset,
your every hope's sunrise.
You show me words no poet
could rival with your eyes.

I light your body's passion,
your breath caught with desire.
You are my only reason,
your kiss my only fire.

Without you there's no living,
for even one day's flame
will stop my heart from dying.
No love could be the same.

TOGETHER ALWAYS

She came suddenly in my life,
her slanted smile and wistful look,
her eager want an open book,
her pages blank, but still a wife
whose other world played on her face,
its warning lost in wild embrace.

Each kiss, each touch might be the last,
our every second infinite,
kept time's long reach from ending it.
We stopped our present turning past,
hands locked in every joining breath,
shocked by each groaning little death.

Just when we find each other's heart
and passion burns away control,
your voice speaks words meant to console,
but moves time on, tears us apart.
We'd touched too deep, become as one,
found space where pleasure's never done.

But I would count my life a waste
if we had never shared this tide
that swept our hearts and rushed inside
our mouths, our sex, swelled with the haste
of time played out in frenzied need
to fill each second with their greed.

There is no chance you can forget
or blur our image with regret.
Love holds my teardrop in your eye
to close each lid; our dream's goodbye
will greet each dawn until we die;
there is no ending, you and I.

INTIMATE CONNECTIONS

I ache to touch your soft-downed hair
and stroke each lustrous silken thread
smooth, as roving fingers spread
and part its tresses, skin laid bare.
Then feel the tiny shiver burn
your back and shoulders as they find
your neck pulled tense, eyes shutter-blind,
lips moistened for the fire they yearn.

Pulling closer with reckless greed
that brings us crushing face to face,
a bruising, frantic dreamed embrace
made real by kissing's pressing need.
Our arms and fingers intertwine
in naked playful dalliance,
though awkward in my ignorance
of pleasing a new valentine.

Your breasts, which had been unaware
of contact through their hidden mesh,
now sense the faintest breath of flesh
that floats across constraints they wear.
Then strain with their abrupt release
to eager hands and pulling lips,
engorged by pinching fingertips
and wanton lust that's slipped its leash.

Drawn down, lips burn as finger-pressed
skin trembles, sensing flimsiness,
inflamed and willing more undress,
silk rasping where it once caressed.
Down where your cutting whisp confines
until the slightest hooking tip
unveils the prize my tongue must sip
and swells each contour it defines.

Lust cascades downwards into flood,
swollen by our exploring fire,
caught in a vice of fierce desire,
a silken wetness gorged with blood.
Our joining like a raging storm,
locked where its epicentre lies
penetrated, as spasm dies,
clasped deep inside our sated form.

Eyes drift apart, connect once more,
beyond postcoital, clammy skin,
suffused with all we've poured within,
two bodies floating to their shore.
Breath slows as touch becomes too keen,
and safer caring gestures mark
the ebbing tide of passions spark,
as words remind where flesh has been.

Then distance parts us once again,
except your breathing in my ear
reminds how close we felt on here
in intimate connected pain.
Desire evoked by speech alone
mere trickery of thought and word;
real touch would make this seem absurd...
but love must sometimes use the phone.

SHAPING MORPHEUS

Nestle close into my shoulder
and hear the stream of conscious,
fluttering wings that brush whisper
my word-craft, shaping Morpheus
with soft hypnotic feather down,
caressing your perfect loving.

Eyes closing with the slightest graze
of moistened lips on care-worn skin,
filling with scent-warm summer days
the emptiness of solitude;
hands trail—entwined in fragrant streams
of sun-sweetened water lilies.

Fold yourself into tomorrow,
where every touch of skin is real,
each blissful shiver returned
with silken butterfly kisses
settling on arm-cradled breasts
bathed in opalescent moonlight.

Breathe my deep-pressed body's rhythm
until there is no difference
between the beating of our hearts,
embracing night's oblivion.
Then in my arms your body keep,
and drift my darling into sleep.

WAKING TO MY LOVE

Soft tendrils of form finger-touch
the beginnings of consciousness.
An image floating, closeted
in the deep recesses of mind,
appearing, disappearing,
drifting on a warm, streaming light,
leaking past fluttering eyelids.
Faster now, a steady presence,
image slowly bringing focus,
eyes opening onto a smile
as lips briefly press their desire
upon a softly waking face.
Your eyes staring up into those
you know have one lifelong message,
which is the tenderness of love.

WHY I LOVE YOU…

I love you for being my day;
I love the crazy things you say.
I love you for being so right;
I love you for my dreams at night.

I love you since I have no choice;
I love your words and sexy voice.
I love you join your lips with mine;
I love your eyes that always shine.

I love your smiles are just for me;
I love you want to set me free.
I love that you can see my soul;
I love you want to make me whole.

I love you more with every kiss;
I love to feel your heartbeat miss.
I love each breast that craves my touch;
I love you wanting me so much.

I love the way you move your hips;
I love your flushed pink oyster lips.
I love you pulling me inside;
I love you have nothing to hide.

I love that you can't say goodbye;
I love your every drawn-out sigh.
I love being *in love* with you;
I love you for loving me too.

I love all that you are to me
and all I'll ever want to be.

OUT OF LOVE

THE RING

I contemplate its presence,
a simple burnished epitaph
caught in an accidental sun,
life empty without a finger.
Name and date still legible,
no longer hidden, pressed
twisting against taut skin,
lying accusingly on the dresser,
untouched, unwanted,
its worn circle etched
with the work of living—
earth, weeds, dishes—
carrots and potato peel.
No more the love
it once encircled,
admiring faces gazing
reflected in the shine
of new spun gold
on entwined fingers
stretched across a lover's table
laid for only two,
clinking against crystal,
champagne flutes
bubbling with promise,
frothed in celebration.
…But now alone,

experience done,
like some scarred fighter
fallen on hard times
punched with the hole
of drunk remembrance.
An ornament of time,
never more worn,
never thrown.
A golden artefact
gathering dusty neglect
and the dull tarnish
of fading memory.

NOTHING TO FORGIVE

Our dreams floated on fairy wings
across gossamer-spun fields brushed
with rose, indigo, and vermillion.
The flowers on Mathew's grave
blooming with fulfilment
of his haunting promise.

You dared first...
stopping breath's question,
answered by impassioned words
and growing imagined touch.
Then the incredible sighs
that shook each fractured soul
and brought our loving's miracle
to banish the spectre
of your expected death...
forever.

Nothing was impossible to us;
nothing could stop our fairy tale,
not even becoming mortal
in a harsh world of pain.
But we were always too late,
a year ago's lifetime
so different in its end.
Your discovery then not us...

though we were your hope.
Another had stolen your heart
and tossed it away,
leaving lost poetic dreams
for me to read when I arrived
and know the savage truth
of your stepfather's hands,
of Mathew's death,
of the baby who stopped
you leaving from the door
that could open another life.

Another life free from
the weight of misplaced love
and the obsessive jealousy
of possession, rape, and violence.
All, for a while, forgotten
in our brief trembling embrace,
forgotten by two souls' willing arms
whose love conjoined in a room
of wistful promises and secrets
far, far away.

Although even as we lay
amongst crushed, fragrant petals
of our final love-making,

the seeds of forced destruction
were growing inside you,
waiting to cry just one word
…"unforgiveable"!

Undying love just the same.
A love to be remembered
in the quiet times
or when faces are touched
by the fingered caress
of sultry summer breeze.
Or a familiar look
found in some stranger's eyes,
the look that reminds,
with tears wiped away,
how it might have been,
two joyful rivers flowing
into a boundless sea,
never to be parted.

Then the final spell, of course,
conjured by the knowing,
knowing there was never
anything to forgive…
"Nothing at all".
It was just the world,

its seeming cruel fate
and impossible circumstance
but powerless in its spite
to crush such love.
Again we will say,
with wishful remorse
and the simplest
of whispered sighs,
"Nothing...nothing at all".

AN UNTIMELY ROMANCE

Yesterday's words forgot your age;
today a doubting caution breaks;
tomorrow's sense is centre stage.
This time there can be no mistakes;
love does not mind whose form it takes.

These words are all that I can use
to weave a careful spell and thrill
those spent emotions, which amuse
the days and nights when time sits still
so you can speak their sounds at will.

Neat lines across a flimsy sheet
spread floating in the spring-flushed air
to touch a faint-impressioned seat,
which knew my shape while yours was there,
flat words transformed by spoken care.

Strange how their threads connect the heart
when little else can cross the way
that keeps our bodies far apart
and moves them further every day
in hope that love won't grow or stay.

What words will this tomorrow bring?
What silent thoughts will moments spend
in hiding truths, whose wavering
will change each day my journey's end,
a sometime partner, lover, friend?

At times just one more final call,
when prose demands a rushed reply,
you crush me with distraction's fall,
a futile object in your sky,
a robin bleeding, left to die.

If planned resolve that each day makes
could alter facts and futile strife,
this searching mind, whose body aches,
would find new truths to fill your life—
beyond the one that makes a wife.

A hopeless case, we might agree,
though one these words will not concede;
once they are born, they live for me,
but feel no pain and cannot bleed,
rhymes your protected heart must read.

AN END TO DREAMING

The dream is gone;
its eyes are open,
staring into an emptiness
that once promised hope,
could skirt the void
of common images
reflected by a sun
grown larger with age
now shaded in eclipse
by the thousand
feathered wings
of escape,
beating their migration
from my heart.

There is no second coming,
no hope of light reborn,
no Phoenix myth to
resurrect the flames
of this last day.
The evening sun
catches each golden leaf
touched or fallen from
breeze-whispered trees

and leads our way
to soft-lit streets
that turn so many corners
with ready, wistful kisses.

Direction unimportant,
mere inconsequence,
but forced between
the warmth of willing lips,
and half closed lids
of deep-accepting eyes.
Wishing we were lost forever,
pleading for another path
that could lead us
back from the edge
of final oblivion.

Hope spinning on a coin,
thrown to wake the sunrise
of a future world
where dreams might come true.
But only landed on its head,
alone with pinched reality
that snuffs out light

in the growing shadow
of this, our final moment's
darkening sunset.

Fallen out of sleep
and woken by the glare
of another risen sun.
Dreams scorched by
the molten heat
of branded truth
that sears our flesh
with raw remembrance of
our present love's goodbye.

THE DEATH OF A ROBIN

He flew with hope of better days,
his heart buoyed with a quickened beat,
his wings catching the golden rays
of sunlight dancing in its heat.

He landed in your garden's tree,
proud that his flight engaged your eye,
and thrilled your future thoughts to see
a constant lover in your sky.

Spring turning summer when we meet,
time stood in dancing pools of light
thrown on a corner of your street
to bathe our final first good night.

Then with the start of autumn chill,
leaves tossing with a sudden squall
show him that permanence might fill
a future grasped by giving all.

But then it seemed another bird
still held the longing in your eye,
his hopes of mutual flight absurd,
fast plummet from an empty sky.

CALM CERTAINTY

I wonder where you are, my love?
Hope resurrects a life each day
with thoughts of us and promise that
this *now* will bring the sudden
shock of revelation into being,
fragrant in its spring of fevered
aromas and writhing spirit
filling the scent of memory
with barbaric lust and wanting.

It haunts each loss my dying
brings to measured breath.
Dying that could say the words
no other mouth could speak—
no other thought could know.
The end so simple in its calm,
pure certainty of purpose,
conveying meaning
to my ebbing life
through spoken truth
...and its consequence.

The loss I found each night
and morning at your door
that opened my existence.
Opened with you there,
smiling at my entrance

into each living mantra
chanted in the quiet that
wandered into evening.
Tied in corners of bustling streets
where neither waited
except to cross the distance
that was placed between us.

Placed so you couldn't hear
the words my heart had
woven through your being.
Caught up in a web
no afterthought could escape,
no previous life could soothe
with familiar comforting.

There is no singing
but the song we made,
together with the sound
that played each chord
into the harmony
of coexistence.
Sound that dying,
in its final breath,
brought more than
living voices ever sung.

INTIMATE STRANGERS

There were many ends
to our relationship…
but never a beginning.
The days stretched out
their hopes of many nights
locked in warm embrace
but realised only once…
and that just into evening,
the sunset shared
one solitary time.

The rest caught up in words,
imaginings, and plans
that turned each empty day
into passages of longing,
each loving page of care
slow reason couldn't read.

How impossible the hope
had become without meeting.
Now slipped too far beyond,
too late to grasp slim chance
that dangled further off.
Far too late to quell

those fateful changes
that will always come
when time spins past
without decisive action.

So reaches this our end,
another end, but final.
An end that found again
no fast beginning, only love
without imagined end,
that cheated us together.
So close, but ever far,
intimate strangers
whose moment never came
but may also never pass.

YOUR FINAL CHOICE

The date is set
for an end...
or a beginning...
or even the end
of a beginning...
time will reveal all.
The decision is made...
I can feel it caught
in your tidy words
and their evasions,
keeping their distance,
even when breaking
ranks to murmur love.
The rest is simply
marking time
and hoping it
will change with
something other
than a fault
that forces choice
of second best
and preludes
an uncertain future
of commitment.

UNDER A BLUE-CLOUDED SKY

Under a blue-clouded sky
We lay and talked,
of certain heaven, you and I.
Even knowing what had seemed
mesmerized in drifting,
stately masses,
azure deep with
puffed-out cheeks,
shape-shifting,
billowing softly
into lazy sleep.

We dreamed reflected shafts of light
that played upon our sheltered eyes
and teased each ribboned hope's delight
with colours of a truth's disguise
in yellow, aspen-fingered blue,
bathed in clinging mountain dew
that's wetter than this upturned face,
etched by each lying teardrop's stain
and promise-broken acid rain,
white kisses of our dead embrace.

LIES

What could we have said
to separate the moments
when lies, no longer trifles,
emerged as a solid truth
behind the shattered mask of
our tomorrow's hope?

Sickening barbs, shortened breath,
nausea sweeping through
the dizziness of deceit.
Self-blame leads to nagging doubt,
trapping foundering resolve
between anger and despair.

So on to confrontation,
willing that another truth
faces down the one we know.
We plead and recriminate
to lance the deeper feeling
that sorry is not enough.

Just simple words spun
out in a cluttered tableau
of all that has passed
and should have led us
to a very different
future life than this.

Shortened syllables
to keep us in brief control
of emotions, clipped, run raw
with regret for losing touch.
Caught in lost realities,
little more than a footnote.

And a short one at that.
The kind that fills
the hidden space
where other words end
and another page begins...
Almost an afterthought.

Now become irrelevant
to this final twisted end,
where we recompose the plot,
sex-numbed back behind the mask,
where older lies cannot ask
questions newer ones forgot.

DROWNED

We are drowning
in the midst of another
tragedy that drags our
helpless corpse
over flinted rocks.
Cruel, storm-raked,
glistening knives
that split our flesh
with savage truth
and whetted blood.
The open wounds
of tortured innocence.

Stirred by restless waves,
two lifeless souls
caught in a sudden shock
of slanting winter sun.
Sucked down, unawares,
into the carefree,
sense-strewn current,
writhing beneath
the boiling flume
and pounding roar
of breaking sea.

Life's savage
surface noise
far distant now.
Just languid,
ebbing emptiness,
stretching down
into crushing gloom
and eternal silence.

So forgive me, darling,
there is no other way
than this cold deep's
escaping breath.
Breath that chokes
its final rise and fall,
as water reaches in
and smothers all.
Starves each living thought
whose feeling spoke
"How much it mattered"—
"How much we cared".

Sense fading with the light
of remembered sunsets
dancing in your eyes,
their bright reflection

dimming what we had,
blunting the twisting
blade of our desire
that brought us love—
at least for a while—
but with this drowning,
stopped the breath
that was the heartbeat
of its existence.

A FINAL SEPARATION

Our time has gone, its hands choked with telling.
Memories where we could not live without
touching, held together with its feeling
of skin tight with belonging, beyond doubt.

Now shattered with forgetfulness, whose lost,
remorseful sentience beggars what we had.
A world of sheer intensity that tossed
your dancing curls and drove my wanting mad.

Still turning every head except for mine,
each bricf absence bringing faint relief
and wonder at its callous anodyne,
not even a moment of passing grief.

All those years of tender care ground to dust,
remembered with vagueness and mystery,
like grains of sand slipping their grasping trust,
falling through faked half truths and misery.

So does the impossible become born,
deformed in its moment of creation,
delivered with a knife, its life air-torn,
lungs screaming parting's last communion.

TIME, DREAMS, AND REALITY

TIME, DREAMS, AND REALITY

Sleep soothe my leaden eyelids,
lest time once more usurp
the timeless world of dream.
Or lead me through the endless streets
past paper stands and offices
that dead seem sadly changed
from the life of commercial day.

The very stillness seems to mock
the chimes of an infernal head
that regulates allotted breath.
The pounding heartbeat of this earth
is chained in a mass of whirling cogs
as lifeless as a piece of rock
that swinging, by an intellectual force,
breaks down a wall
as inanimate as itself
and returns from its destructive work
a slowly turning chunk of stone, no more.

THE PRESS OF TIME

Dream of the passing press of time
that leads minds to oblivion.
Not forgotten by emotion
but wary of all heads that chime
the counted hours lost in my mind,
searching for truth I could not find.

LOST DREAMS

It's morning, even though it shouldn't be.
Clocks can be such fretful, loving deceivers
that tempt unwilling bodies losing sleep,
waking my dreams with euphoric musings,
scattering reason's secure history.
Thoughts pulled taut by some invisible strings,
dancing, reeling, staggering out of tune,
controlled by nothing but the hands of time.

Does each minute now equal a minute
when my eyes flutter behind their lids
to dream-sleep such fantastical visions?
No surely I'm released from time's constraints.
Nothing seems fixed or even tangible,
except the flickering numbers on its face.

So where are they now, all those time-lost dreams
I should have had if dark and light were distinct
instead of numbered equal on a changeless dial?
Will they come again tomorrow,
jostling with evening's promise
of sleep's normality?
Or will they simply escape dimension,
a scattered constellation of images

locked in their single moment
out of measured time,
between the realms of fantasy and truth,
fixed in that space between brain and mind
where nothing moves to trouble consciousness?

GRADUATION

One by one they come,
their bright young faces
shy, laughing, arrogant,
but filled with the promise
of youthful ambition.
A room full of dreams,
stifled by the constraints
of formal education.

Eyes glassy with hope
of far greater things
than on this battered stage,
where names are called
to summon their presence
into the stark yellow light.

They applaud each measured
word of congratulation.
Favourites clapped
on just a mention,
while others weave
their long passage
in a slow, whispered silence
of lesser consequence.

Though all stiff with pride
and the warmth of
inspirational speech
that theirs is the next
generation of hope.

I am greeted on their stage
with nervous practised words
and clammy hands.
Eyes confronting
with shy embarrassment
or casual disdain.
Slouched ill-hanging suits
with shirttail tongues
or dresses spilling
abandoned constraint…
expectation uncovered
on every upturned face.

Then, finally alone,
this Duty done.
Gifted flowers
uncomfortably cradled.
Thoughts turned in

so history can trace
the thousand
imagined lives
their future
might embrace.

NEW YEAR

The year draws
to a thankful end,
its last days tipped
with the spur
of urgent celebration
and slowing body
grown fat with the weight
of larded history,
gorged with that
endless conundrum
of wanting more
than we can have...
or even deserve.
Now slim again with
a New Year's hope
some other feast
brings gastronomic pleasure
and consumptive success,
without exercise,
without the stored calories
of circumstance and failure
that serve only fast food into
life's constant begging bowl.

NOT JUST ANOTHER PASSING YEAR

Today seems likely it will forget all others,
spawned alone in thought, without sisters or brothers.
It is new born, full of hope that slowly smothers
years passed in fevered care of shallow ambition,
cast off as new life fosters anticipation.
Tomorrow's image, cast beyond its reflection,
knows in that instant where future clarity lies,
counted older by the world but younger by eyes
that see what can't be seen in time's numbered disguise.

BEYOND JUDGMENT
AND DEATH

JUDGMENT

What is it that they know—
or think they know?
Some cataclysmic truth
scheduled to be revealed
in the next commercial break?

A thirty-second wonder,
pithed through its body
with sharpened conceit,
strung together with
beads of shredded flesh,
wired impertinence
gouging the straining neck,
bearing weak platitudes
with false simplicity,
simpering from its art.

Gaping mouths pouting
choked-off mimicry,
gagged from utterance
of some final truth.

Then the drop that snaps
and fashions dancing limbs
plummeted into nothing,

dangling on a taut string,
death's hung consequence
removed from opinion
below life's centre stage.

PORTRAIT OF A DYING CHILD

She turned away,
but with the autumn gloom,
presented more than just a face
of diminished hope and finite grace.
I turned as if to grasp
the faintness of one hopeful gesture,
but all seemed useless,
time and space
frozen in the doubting pose of
callous death's sharp twisted guile.
But those who saw remember well
her final passing moment's smile.

LIFE IN A MATERIAL WORLD

Forbidden cloister echoes
whisper to an unknown shrine,
where sits a fitted demigod,
a hoard of apples in his desk,
who calls the hooded masses
to crawl before a burnished throne
and cleave the air with nonsense
to benefit a future brood
whose infant squalor reeks of sense
but only speaks of life as food.

CONTEMPLATING BUDDHA

Locked in eternity of mind,
he sits, half paradise in chains,
the smiling master of the game,
and meditates upon the stone,
which gave him form without design,
hands clasped in his eternal sign.

His presence goes beyond all art;
no human artifice remains;
pure spirit lifts each bowing head;
compassion characters each face.
All thought transcends his worldly shrine,
his way both human and divine.

IMMORTAL IN ICE

This living goes on after all,
the thankless opportunity
and spirit of chaotic dreams
drifting across Antarctic seas.
So why should anything matter
in this bleak frozen spectacle
caught up in peaks of burning ice
or that I should die here and leave
no shadow in a wilderness
unmindful of my life's passing?
Though remnants remain suspended,
my spirit's call shall not live on,
but frozen out of time, will drag
its echo down into the deep,
not life in death, but death in sleep.

VOICES

Another day's clamoured silence,
willing that all humanity's noise
will find its single voice again
and touch this empty, growing quiet
that passes for a sounding life.

Words pulled into knots by questions,
no tidy answers ever found,
unravelled by some busy truth
whose fingers might seem so certain
in pointing to the ceiling's crack,
which flaws each careworn perspective.

Running through unbroken visions
on painted shrouds of empty white
that canopy my pounding head.
This snaking, damaged purpose
enfolds me in its sleeping coils.

A striking hand to snuff the light
so I can dream a venomed sleep
and suffocate with scaly rings
those dark enticing hooded shapes
that hide another beckoned call.
Each whisper mute from breath's mistake,
a thousand deaths before I wake.

ON DEATH

Here
surrounded by thoughts that
shroud the drunken precipice,
which drags me, nightly,
to this lonely vigil,
I return to my childhood.
I stand, a tottering infant,
swaying at the crumbling edge
and, wrapped in nothing
but the clinging mist
that serves both to entice,
and to obscure
the depths my mind can reach.

What if I should fall
and plunge through all
the episodes that go to make a life…
What then?
Will suddenly all be clear?
Will there remain no questions
to employ the thousand
spinning moments,
which contemplate with me
the callous face of death?

For fall one day I must
and put a final end
to curiosity…
No more than that,
much more…
A final end to this
consumptive passion
that warns me to exist
at any price.

Is he down there?
That I can't be sure.
Not just a pile of bones
to gesture gross deceit
with outstretched fingers.
Is he down there?...
Call him what you will,
waiting for infirmity
to shake my careful balance
on the edge of living—
pulling me gently down
to meet my fate.

Still, each night,
I am left to hope that
when the final moment comes,

no questions will remain to swell
the doubts that rise with every mist,
and nothing will disturb
a silent mind
grown old,
grown tired.
Then, contented,
I can suck the dark, thin,
rushing air,
which limits me
one fleeting breath
before my death.

WHERE LIFE IS STILL

Silence is coming;
hear still the water drip down on the window sill,
the brook's joyful murmur, soon lifeless and dull;
man must remain with the beast and the fowl.
The birds have no feathers on Calvary hill—
grief everlasting.

Yet he is here,
watching me creep with a terrified care
to peer into silence through frost-blackened glass
at nature's stagnation and dew-frozen grass,
mouthing my question—"What happened there?"
Eye sheds a tear.

Silence is come.
No more creak the hinges of ageing doors
and crosses bear witness to Calvary's dead,
suspending forever humility's head.
Blank pages now stand for political laws,
and we are dumb.

MONASTERY

They shuffle—formless—
old habits and worn cloth.
Grey spectres floating
across a marbled sea,
cold in the stifling heat
of summer afternoon.
Their dragging footfall
echoing through vaulted,
stone-scaped arches.

The dwindling keepers
of an artisaned leviathan,
crafted with common blood,
hung with nightmare frescoes
and transcendent faces of
glorified human suffering.

Speaking hope of tongues
in hallowed whispers,
turning to dogmatic,
baleful chants
that sound a bygone age
where all believed
an impossible truth,

even when flooded
with the soul
of fermented grape.

Or fallen silent
in the hope of inner
peace and sanctity
that robs the senses
of that other world
we all inhabit.

We hear the hollow chanted
song in practised tones
of ancient runes,
beckoning from shadow
but move towards
another, newer truth,
whose knowledge
of the hidden self
rejects such emptiness.

Turns to the labour
of hard experience
and each moment's
safety of achievement.

Escapes with us
back into the sun's
warm smell of pine
and red-baked earth.
The more certain heat
of life's essential flame.

THE PRIEST

Tomorrow when a new dawn breaks,
I'll tell the world how I am one
who learns from each of his mistakes
and stands when other mortals run.
Now today I find I must elude
the serpent whose annoying sin
disturbs my peaceful solitude
and snap when I should usher in
a throng of patient penitents.
Just how can one still find the space
for free will in so cramped a place
as mind that worships and repents
to a God who created it to be
self-centred for eternity?

LAZARUS

Midnight toiling through a graveyard,
brittle shadows leaping
through impossible resurrection,
laughing in the light of one dim candle,
falters, as one faint staccato clack
of bones bleached with remembrance
calls up Lazarus, crawling backwards,
harried through lost generations
dancing wild with rotten rags.
Flying round a creaking gibbet,
their hollow rattle points the compass,
returns less mute with hanging flesh
to tell us of his fabled grave
then crumples in one jointless heap,
their secrets locked in sainted relics
prolong eternal discourse.

HOPE LOST AND REGAINED

HATS IN THE LOOKING GLASS

Unwelcome truths slip in between
age-twisted thoughts of what has been
or might be…if we just could break
those ancient knots of each mistake.

Though real mistakes will always be
the ones we made but didn't see,
with life so blinkered, busied round
safe comfort's rose glow-tinted ground.

It once was easy to believe
dreams threaded onto dreaming's sleeve,
but that was then, and we were young,
clothes bright and fit, not drab and hung.

What, when you dress the other side,
youth's colours in their wardrobe hide,
turned inside out, they can't be seen,
dreams hooked in stitches on each seam.

Better by far the needle's end
than platitudes no point can mend,
or ready suits the dreary find
to scarecrow-hang old-fashioned mind.

What enterprise in living dead,
with nothing tailored for your head?
No fabric for you to retain,
just what you've lost and can't regain.

There is no future under grass…
Put on a hat! Look in the glass!
Turn down the brim; see how it sits—
Or find a better one that fits.

Then wake the day; give birth a shout!
Another closet life come out!
Wear what naked truths you must
but shed old cloth and coffin dust.

GOOD FRIDAY

The daylight's firstborn, fleeting cry,
winged feathers beating night-choked sky,
pierced with its urgent song
to rouse a drunken thief
who's stolen time to find relief
from prayers striking this morning's gong.

Where are those caring tongues who, free,
spoke promised endless love for me?
Closed safe by other clocks,
their chimes pretending mind
will make up time safe hearts can't find
in busied lives snapped tight with locks.

There is no prophet for this day
to curb the pain or make life stay.
Just sense of death that brings
its knowing, sure, unkind,
without history to rewind
past notes this dying always sings.

No resurrection now can come,
no Sunday's hope, no stone undone;
no miraculous end,

no fierce apocryphal cry
to speak one final truth's goodbye
and turn each silent, absent friend.

For I have seen them all through eyes
far brighter than these morning skies,
each nascent thought and breath
of hope stripped bare before
my foot trod naked on their shore.
Those times of love still beggar death.

LOST HOPE

They say hope is for dreamers
whose truth rose-colours trust,
with visions blurred by fevers
burned into urns of dust.

Dust that once built cities
now grains in desert sands
that flow with shifting eddies
and slip through outstretched hands.

It's not that hope's capricious;
her choice, which once seemed free,
this summer turned mendacious
and then abandoned me.

Maybe in depths of winter,
she'll flurry warmth with snow
and melt the frosted arbour
that's closed my heart below.

And with each changing season,
there will be other dreams,
but none where truth or reason
won't dam the spring-tide streams.

Where once a childlike magic
could light each waking day,
hope's music now seems tragic,
except when others play.

LIFE PASSING BY

Do rescue me from all this care
of life passing by my window.
I choke here, while it breathes pure air,
heart pounding with its rush and flow,
a quickened pulse I cease to know;
my hopeful blood has ebbed to slow,
its warmth turned cold to mountain snow.
Limbs frozen from that moment where
eyes opened with unseeing stare,
chilled by frost of glazed despair—
none living now will join me there.

THE HOLLOW MEN

Night's crush is come again,
its coil-sprung fingers
close around my vitals,
skin white and bloodless,
clammy, emptied by fear.
There seems no end
to these nothing hours
between sleep and waking.
The animus of a mind
tormented by *what-ifs*
crowding each second thought
with writhing panic
and aimless purpose.

Nor is there time
to sense a knowing end…
just infinity of pain,
eating slowly into dawn
whose light hungers action
and turns the clock again
towards some conclusion.
Each morning's step closer
to the welcomed moment
of resolution…
whatever that might be.

Beyond helpless despair,
some primal evolution
bringing welcome change
to sterile nights filled
with sweat-coupled dreams.
Encircled instead by the arms
of a mother soul,
whose loving warms
the earth with my existence.

Then I will know the course
that can turn the path
of hollow men
who seek my fall
but have no other life
than in my end.
In truth, no life at all
beyond the echo of
of their shallow footsteps
sounding gross deceit
upon my back.

BREAKING FREE

Sultry evening shadows stretch languid form,
shrugging off working cloth of shackled day.
Their lightened step escapes the growing storm
of weighted thought and naked sombre grey.

Cares etched in ashen face and drawn-out lips,
left where they lie awaiting each new turn
that twists old truth as worn existence slips
and slides into wet of newborn concern.

Cocooned by myth of water breaking free,
hopes bathed in a cloudburst whose sudden birth
gathers into pools of a twilight sea,
sucked slowly back into forgetful Earth.

ABANDONING FAMILIAR SOUNDS

In that moment, we abandoned
care of all that we've gathered round.
Our present lives, so moribund,
give comfort in their steady sound,
familiar in middle tones
that please with easy listening.
Our nights spent wandering alone
in places past imagining,
where something empty resonates,
its vessel walls constraining need.
But can such hollow music make
our lives full by denying greed?
No we are not half-formed muses,
warmly cocooned in single beds;
there is more than conscience chooses
to play our hearts and lose our heads.

SECOND SIGHT

Earth spins, miasmic
in watery eye
and fluming breath.
Cold etching into lines
of tears that sting
my icy cheeks,
blushed with wintry hoar.

Steps press their marks
on a virgin floor
and state my purpose
to arrive, but where?
There is scarce sense
to know or care.
Only sunlight,
washing in its flood
of copper-yellow
shafted beams
the pit my worries
held in darkened,
grey-capped shadows,
clouding their intent.

My heavy carcass
dragged useless thoughts

out of their closed,
familiar coffin
that's buried days
with sucking earth
nailed down into years.
Now forgotten
in this coloured stream,
flowing with its tones
and hues of vibrant light
that dance their naked feet
upon my erstwhile grave.

Up where no earth
remembers when
I laughed or cried
or slept or dreamed
into clear air,
revived, complete,
that second sight
this morning's soul
awoke with light.
So every turn
and path I take
my weary steps
no longer trace

worn intention
with deceit...
A world grown honest
under my feet.

HOME

This is my country;
no other place
brings tranquillity
like her welcome face.
Her battered shore,
her restless sea,
a vital claw
locked into me,
which twists a knot
so deep inside
it cannot
ever be untied.

So familiar
but never dull,
its seasons stir
the sleeping lull
of meadow grass
and forest leaves,
dew-lapped they toss
in casual breeze.

Its rolling downs
and wicker gates,
small market towns,
tumbledown estates.

Its village greens
and maypole fairs,
outdated scenes
tradition spares.

Grey castles steeped
in murder's stain,
worn smooth by feet
and constant rain
that wets each crown
with cups of tea,
drunk sitting down
communally.
And flat, warm beer
served jugged or straight
to ordered queues
whose trains are late.
Where talk of weather
remains in vogue,
inconstance fleeter
than a shifty rogue.

Where willow prods
its measured stroke,
a game of odds
time seems to choke.

Fierce umpired calls
make tourists stare
at green-baize battles
fought on a square.
But do they guess
each boundary gained
is one war less
and peace retained?

Sun drives us naked
to the beach,
skin unschooled,
whiter than bleach,
blushed raw and angry
by a feckless sun.
Mad dog jamboree
or lemming-run?

Now in the quiet
of evening sun,
the fading light
as day is done,
my spirit's free
as a seagull's cry.
Here I must be
and here will die.

WHAT AM I?

What am I?
A gritted speck
lodged in the slitted eye
of streaked infinity,
ignorant of its blindness
but pricked by its pain?
My mind's shining tapetum
jaundiced with insight's store
of collected fading light,
revealing each predator
caught by my slightest,
fear-practiced glance.

Or am I a dusty attic,
found empty by all
except for one dark corner,
damp from a broken tile?
Piled with the shrink-packed
detritus of yesterdays.
The stored slime-mould of
collective experience
where the deep past has died
of deprivation and starvation
but cannot shake the drip
of rainfall's memory
bathing each hard,

forgotten mistake
with the slippery life
of new born guilt.

Or am I the slow ache
that never leaves
my crowded head
as it lies too long still
on a cold, foot-worn stair?
The stair that marks the limit
of where feet and hands
have crawled on bloodied knees.
The stair I curl up on,
its comfort foetus-safe,
its knowledge cocooned
but wondering still
if the stairway
has any purpose
but its climbing?

Is it time to go on?
Do I dare stand and ask
so many questions?
What truth am I?
What must I become
to reveal the answer

whose knowing brings
the lasting peace of
absolute certainty?

Is it in that feeling
that the world is shrunk
to just two,
and in the urgent,
consuming need
of those two
becoming one?
Does it lie there
in the nestled warmth
of a soft-pillowed neck,
pulse throbbing gently,
pale skin damp and slick,
its pores suffused
with the aftermath
of frantic loving?

Or in the tearing wonder
ripping through the cord
that could once contain
each beat of my heart
with the shocked sound
of a firstborn's purple cry,

as he takes his first breath,
and sucks his first teat
that ushers warm demand
of lifelong love
and willing dependence?

Or in the cool breeze
raising the down
on naked, bloodless skin,
hackled and pricked
with anticipation,
as the ice-wolf prepares
to launch its final strike
and rip out the vitals
of my body's warmth?

Or in the discovery
that makes sense
of the impenetrable,
that turns the universe
into just another
small backyard
hung with washing
and echoing the
simple innocence
of children's voices?

A compelling truth
to threaten understanding
and replace the hollow,
ignorant sound
of slavish nonsense
that gives no comfort
to a questioning mind.

Perhaps all…
and yet none of these.
There is no answer
but the living
and the waking
from thirsty sleep.
Eyes and feet
turning each corner
as if the answer
will lie etched
on the smooth pavement
or in the rain falling
from a cloudless sky
or in knowing
there is nothing
at the rainbow's end
but the simple pot
of my existence.

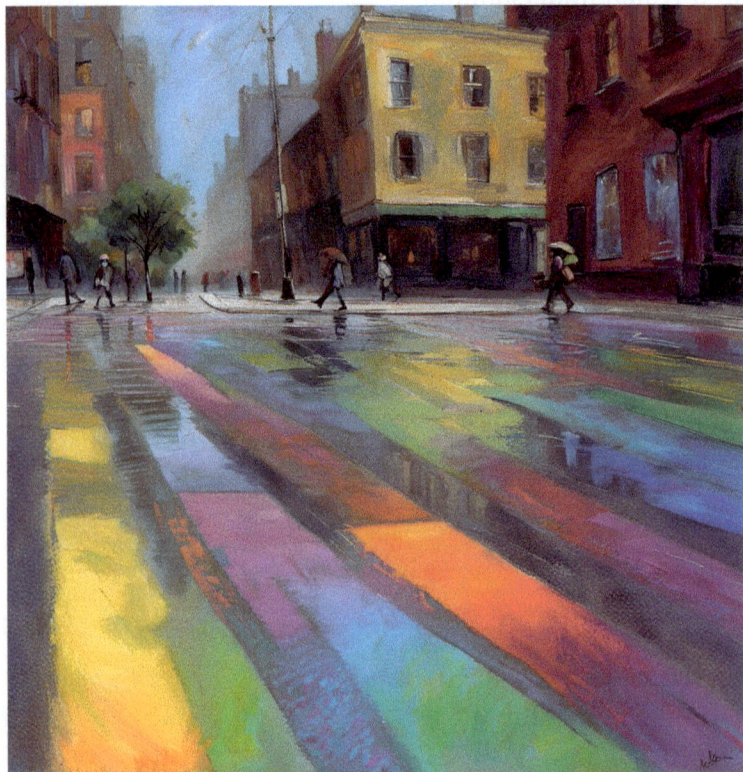

MIND GAMES AND CONFLICTS

A SCHIZOPHRENIC MIND

The circle first began today,
wheeling through a time vault
age of excremental care
to vomit on a stage of eyes
preserved in faultless memory,
meaning cast in an artefact
that called itself a life.
Half-formed spectres shuffling the void,
remnants of a callous world
lost in the vagrancy of hope
that lured them to a stage
for this performance.
Who would witness a façade,
so wasted on a ring of skulls
cracked where the bullet entered?
Entered where the final dream
was nothing but a passing thought.
Split where intention lay awake
and thudded on through conscience,
guilt, or periodic shame
before the stage went black.
Black before applause could break
through all the empty sockets
peering through the footlights.
Black before the eyes regained
composure from the studied mime.

Black as the curtain dropped
and called for one momentous pause
before the second act began.
Blacker still for its finale,
the division light extinguished
cuts off the player from the play
and darkness fills with voices.
Then will the blind present—
"A Schizophrenic Mind".

MEETING OF MINDS

It's knowing you're distinct from me
that starts this social mystery,
where senses and our memory
combine in mental imagery
to form attraction chemistry.

A shared perception I can tell,
but you've a keener sense of smell
and have some other parts as well,
in thought of which I often dwell,
that ring my hope's arousal bell.

And even if we don't agree,
a conjoined future we can see
but know disputed history
you'll sometimes throw right back at me
when our opinions disagree.

It only takes the slightest clue
for me to know what you might do,
because my mind has been there too,
your life, or mine, one mental view;
I look like me but see like you.

One mind, in theory, binds us two...
So where the hell can I find you?

THE DROWNING POOL

Silver cool Lethean water,
slows all air-sucked thought
with the measured metronome
of sweeping, carving limbs.
The echo of each dipping arm
a vibrating metallic strip,
whose muffled resonance
mind-weaves with eerie rhythm,
the rush of steady silence,
which punctuates each memory's
clamoured discord.

Here remembered syllables are blurred,
the distorted utterance of words
lost in disembodied diphthong,
except those formed inside my head,
mouthed without utterance.
Flashed, shimmering sunlight jewels
crisscross the smooth white glaze
which slides beneath my body's wake,
and all those suppressed distractions
flood into detached consciousness.
A world of sense-transmuted flesh,
that's full-immersed with

dragging, floating-lilied touch
and light diffused by muted sound
in one free-flowing,
synaesthetic stream.

Truth found in a myriad of bubbles
plucked from the surface air.
Soul wrapped in the warm-bathed
spirit of amniotic birth,
drifting without need or purpose
towards another twisted turn,
where lies and self-deception
show minds have no such boundaries.
Their drowning-pools
won't let you live
to puke a second chance of air
this side of sanity.

FALLING

I am falling, pieces of my life
spiralling downwards in lines
of perfect chimney bricks
that should be crusted black
with burnt-out experience.
Though somehow stark and new,
like a cartoon or sanatorium,
where nothing seems to age
from the dirt and blood
of polluting humanity.
There seems no end to the falling
or to the crowd of numbers
filling my calculating mind.
Numbers that won't add or subtract
to find a sum that matters,
their solution lost to an infinity
of recurring nightmares.

DEMONS

They come from where you least expect;
their secrets hide in truth's neglect;
their cancer chokes your tortured soul
with buried fears you can't control
and grows until all hope has left,
their faces many, stark, bereft.

PATCHES

It started when
the coat was almost new,
caught on rust-streaked spikes
of a school-ground prison...
Patches!
Invisible at first.
Perhaps a second pocket
or designer label?
No one suspected
hidden damage.
But the scar remained,
quickly joined by
brothers, sisters,
uncles, cousins,
until finally strangers
thrust their opinions,
and other more physical
appendages
through its crumpled fabric,
until patches and coat
became indistinguishable.

THE CHALLENGES OF AGE

TAP, TAP…

Tap, tap…breaks the weary dream
I've fought each waking night
of sleep that wanders to its end.

Tap, tap…more insistent now,
as light seeps past each cautious lid
and slowly rouses consciousness.

Tap, tap…feathers drum the glass
with urgent lack of etiquette,
that peers with beaded eyes
and yellow breast into my room…
It seems I'm still alive!
Staring at this greeting thrust
of life launched at my windowpane.
Her knowing, in each darting look,
her question-struck, coquettish pose,
held, until exploded flight
lifts her to a blossomed sky
bursting with the laden plumes
of billowed, sun-tipped clouds
that drift in stately fields
of shimmering topaz.

Up where the sunlight
dances to the vibrant noise
of crowded, beating, bodied-wings
and fills each jaded, care-worn sense
with purpose to survive.

Still, tap, tap…deep inside my head
reminds me, as I leave my bed,
one day she'll come and find me dead.

THE CHANGELING

How far to the nearest toilet?
Can I get there in time?
Sleep annoyingly punctuated
by the irresistible need to go
but not knowing if the urge
can be relieved when I get there!
Should I wear diapers?
Twelve undignified pricks
and the worst confirmed.
Unmanned by medication
in a new menopausal world of
hot flashes, tears, care, and indecision,
changing who I was into
an impotent, childlike eunuch
devoid of that remorseless drive
omnipresent for some sixty years.
In some ways a welcome release,
in others a profound disturbing sense
of becoming another alien me.
More likeable, more caring perhaps,
but different at the familiar core.
Expected to maintain the original
as a sham that may never reemerge.
Beneath veneered, noble sophistication,
we are truly wired by blood and piss,
primitive as we have always been

but willing to endure the cost
of a medicated changeling existence
to complete, or support, or simply delay
confronting the ultimate question.

I AM NOT OLD

"I am not old!"
though people say,
"His smile's worn cold!"
"His hair's gone grey!"
Still locked inside
a boy remains
who will not hide
his foolish aims,
who cannot see
the way I look.
"That can't be me,
a lie, a crook?"

Lost, maybe dreams
whose youthful face
saw hopes in streams
where salmon race.
Driven by love…

that's now long gone…

whose silken glove
my heart put on
and once had found
a partner's hand,
but time unwound
that Gorgon's band.

"I am not old!",
though every day
love's promised hold
keeps death at bay.
So when the best
of me is run,
then I can rest,
migration done.

People will say,
"He wanted more!"
"He lost his way!"
"Became unsure."
And who's to know?
They could be right;
progress is slow,
success so slight,
much slipped away
I've looked upon…
But for today,
my boy goes on.

LOSING IT

So have we met, my love, or not?
Your eyes look so familiar;
your voice seems not dissimilar,
but just to whose I've plumb forgot?

Each day is freshly painted new,
but on a canvas that is old.
At least that's how the scenes unfold
with this damned sense of déjà vu.

A past confused, confined to now;
I try to speak as if I know.
No sense of time, though wits run slow,
obsessed with who and where and how?

DEMENTIA

Where did they go, those crowded years,
whose memory swims yesterday
but sinks with slowly reasoned time?
Fretful promises holding tears,
shed for some reason that won't stay,
lost deep in vague euphoric rhyme,
decay replacing words with mime.

Sporadic movement, choke-caught breath,
which hopes the surface-rushing world
will now be somehow calmed by kind,
absented thoughts of certain death
that resurrect through winds unfurled
by doubts wrapped round an ageing mind;
claws crush all vital sparks they find.

Tearing deeper through heat-shocked sheets,
worn thinner by premonition
that loosens hold on everything.
A folded past of tidy pleats
kept fast in tight recollection
of stories changed with remembering,
truths turned lies, just by their telling.

THE SPIT OF AGE

Quiet calls in silence
that mouths each day.
Caught with its food,
choking on the wit
that cuts each moment
of digestive care.

Words ruminating
with unspoken tones,
their broken syllables
and fractured rhyme
disguising meaning…
or perhaps there was none…
none minded, at least.
Just simple drooling sounds
to wet a slack jaw
bathed in incontinence.

An ageing mentor
whose careful advice
loses pique from the spit
which drowns each word
and suffocates the air
that lies in between.
The audience listens
but does not hear

the fallen consequence
that once formed sense
from ready lips.

Now dissolved
in pathos and despair,
mind drowning in its
spattered pools
of failing memory.

FLATLINING

I lie here robbed of sense and breath.
A mannequin whose husklike shroud
awaits the flatline call of death,
the mirror clear of living's cloud.

The curtain drawn around in haste
to cover what might shock again,
a gesture from my breathless waste,
restore each whispered thinking pain.

One bends to listen to the croak
that babbles from each pulsed display,
their effort causing phlegm to choke
the last words I would want to say.

"Don't ask to follow certain men.
Their truths lie only closed, not brave.
Find through uncertainty the pen
that writes of hope beyond my grave."

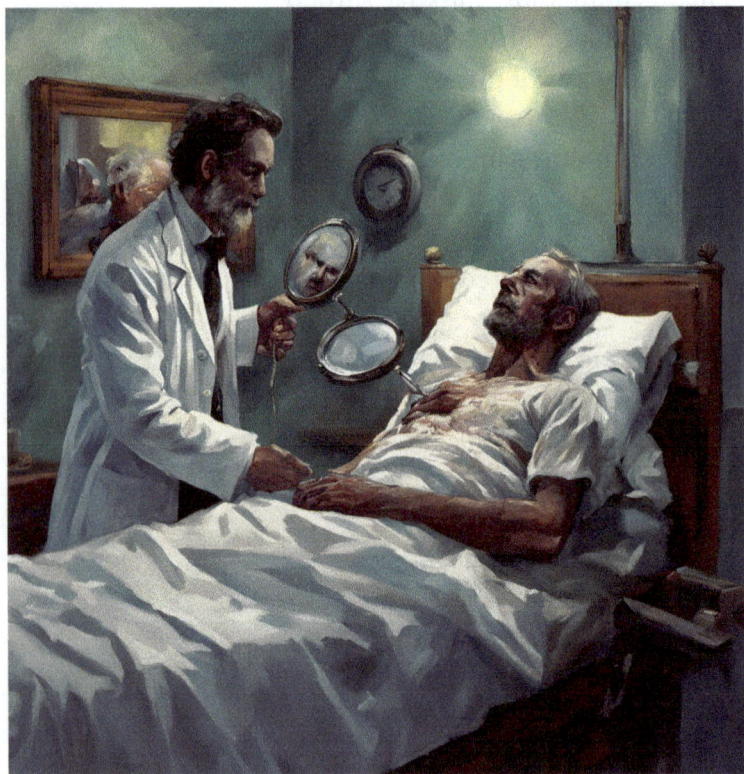

ABOUT THE AUTHOR

Professor Keith Kendrick was born in London in 1954. He left school at sixteen to pursue a career in advertising in London for several years but subsequently decided to gain university entrance. He received his first and doctoral degrees in psychology from the University of Durham in England in 1976 and 1979, respectively, and published his first two scientific papers in *Science* (1979) and *Nature* (1980). During his studies, he moved from the arts to the social science faculty and finally to the science faculty, having first opted in his first year to major in English and philosophy. After holding research or lecturing posts in the University of Durham, Institute of Zoology in London, and University of Cambridge, he spent most of his scientific career working at the Babraham Institute in Cambridge, England, from 1986 to 2011, researching how the brain controls social and emotional behaviours and memory. In 2011, he moved to Chengdu in China as a state-recruited expert professor for the University of Electronic Science and Technology of China, where he is focussed on developing therapies to help with social problems in young children with autism, following discoveries he made while working in the UK. He has

published over three hundred scientific papers, including many in the most prestigious general science and psychiatric journals. His work has also attracted considerable media coverage around the world and has been featured in several television documentaries. Before leaving the UK, he gave over twenty public lectures in the city of London after being appointed professor of physic (medicine) at Gresham College. These have all been on the subject of how the brain controls behaviour in both humans and other species and are available on the web at www.gresham.ac.uk. The ancient Gresham College was founded in 1597 by Sir Thomas Gresham, the then Lord Mayor of London, to inform the business community of new knowledge discovered in the arts, humanities and religion, law, commerce, and science. Previous professors have included the celebrated architect, Sir Christopher Wren, and scientist, Robert Hooke. In China, Professor Kendrick received the highest award given to foreigners in 2019: The International Friendship Award.